Other giftbooks in this series
Go Girl!
Sorry
Little things mean a lot

Published simultaneously in 2005 by Helen Exley Giftbooks in Great Britain
and Helen Exley Giftbooks LLC in the USA.

Illustrations © Caroline Gardner Publishing, Liz Smith and Helen Exley 2005
Text copyright – see page 78
Selection and arrangement copyright © Helen Exley 2005
The moral right of the author has been asserted.

ISBN 978-1-90513-075-7 | 12 11 10 9 8 7

Edited by Helen Exley
Pictures by Liz Smith and Caroline Gardner

Printed in China

Helen Exley Giftbooks, 16 Chalk Hill, Watford, Herts WD19 4BG, UK
www.helenexleygiftbooks.com

A HELEN EXLEY GIFTBOOK

I love you madly

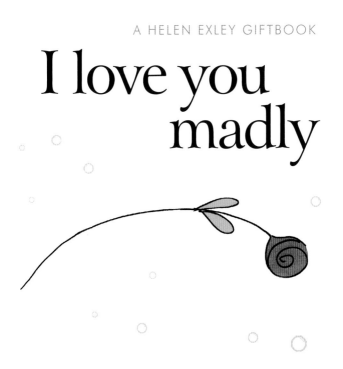

I WANDERED LOST IN YESTERDAY,
WANTING TO FLY,
BUT SCARED TO TRY.
THEN SOMEONE LIKE YOU FOUND
SOMEONE LIKE ME.
AND SUDDENLY, NOTHING
IS THE SAME.

LESLIE BRICUSSE

I love you as one must love:
excessively, to the point
of madness and despair.
There are two things
which must never be mediocre:
poetry and love....
Look upon me as a creature
stricken by a fatal malady....

JULIE DE L'ESPINASSE
(1732-1776)

I see only you,
think only of you,
touch only you,
breathe you,
desire you,
dream of you;
in a word,
I love you!

JULIETTE DROUET
(1806-1883)

You make me glad
to be alive.

STUART AND LINDA MACFARLANE

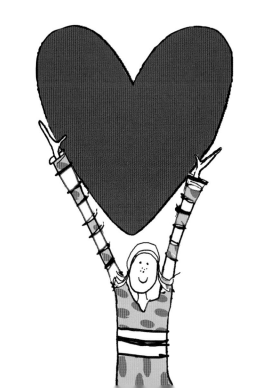

I am mad, I am beside myself!
   I no longer know what I'm doing.
I no longer think of anything.
   What a woman!
               Sarah... Sarah...
when shall I see you again?
I weep, I tremble, I grow mad,
      Sarah I love you!

PIERRE LOÜYS

You have intensified
all colours,
heightened all beauty,
  deepened all delight.
I love you more than life,
  my beauty, my wonder.

SIR ALFRED DUFF COOPER (1890-1954),
TO HIS FUTURE WIFE DIANA

*Woman, in your laughter
you have the music
of the fountain of life.*

RABINDRANATH TAGORE
(1861-1941)

Your words
are as necessary to me
as the sunlight and air....
Your words
are my food,
your breath my wine –
you are everything
to me.

SARAH BERNHARDT
(1844-1923)

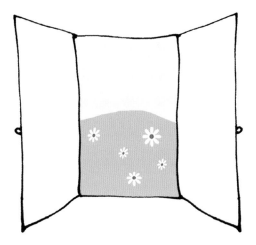

All these years I have found
my pleasures in a thousand things –
   but now you open them anew for me.
I see them through your eyes –
   as well as through my own,
   hear them with a new intensity.
The stage is bright, the dance
   more magical, the trees, the sea,
   the mountains, have taken on
   a new life.

CHARLOTTE GRAY, B.1937

I do love you...
as the dew loves the flowers;
as the birds love the sunshine;
as the wavelets love the breeze.

MARK TWAIN (1835-1910)

I love you, darling.
I don't know of any other way
to put it except that same
old time-worn phrase.
But I do. And I always will.
Nothing can change that.
Not war, nor fire nor flood.
You'll always be part of me
and I you....
I love you, darling. Love you,
love you.

ANNA BEADLE,
TO HER HUSBAND CLINTON

...And I will make thee
beds of roses
And a thousand
fragrant posies.

CHRISTOPHER MARLOWE
(1564-1593),
FROM "THE PASSIONATE SHEPHERD TO HIS LOVE"

I never knew that
I could feel such wonder.
I never knew that love
could be like this.

LESLIE BRICUSSE

Your heart is an inexhaustible spring,
you let me drink deep,
it floods me, penetrates me, I drown.

GUSTAVE FLAUBERT (1821-1880),
TO LOUISE COLET

I have placed my head and my heart
On the sill of the door of my love.
Step gently, child!

TURKOMAN LOVE SONG

I am nearly mad about you,
as much as one can be mad:
I cannot bring together two ideas
that you do not interpose yourself
between them.
I can no longer think
of anything but you.

STUART AND LINDA MACFARLANE

I love you soulfully and bodyfully,
properly and improperly,
every way that a woman can be loved.

GEORGE BERNARD SHAW
(1856-1950),
TO ELLEN TERRY

...I love thee to the level
of every day's
Most quiet need, by sun
and candle-light....
...I love thee with the breath,
Smiles, tears, of all my life!...

ELIZABETH BARRETT BROWNING
(1806-1861)

When I send thee
a red, red rose, –
The sweetest flower
on earth that grows!
Think, dear heart,
how I love thee....

FRIEDRICH RÜCKERT

Here are fruits, flowers,
leaves and branches.
And here is my heart
which beats only for you.

PAUL VERLAINE (1844-1896)

I feel foolish and happy as soon as I let myself think of you. I whirl round in a delicious dream in which in one instant I live a thousand years. What a horrible situation! Overcome with love, feeling love in every pore, living only for love, and seeing oneself consumed by griefs, and caught in a thousand spiders' threads.

HONORÉ DE BALZAC (1799-1850),
TO HIS FUTURE WIFE EVELINA

My feet shall run because of you

My feet shall dance because of you

My heart shall beat because of you

My eyes see because of you

My mind thinks because of you

And I shall love because of you.

AUTHOR UNKNOWN
FROM "ESKIMO LOVE SONG"

I love you
as you are.
Love me
the self-same way.

PAM BROWN, B.1928

...You came,
and the sun came after,
And the green grew
golden above;
And the flag-flowers
lightened with laughter,
And the meadow-sweet
shook with love.

ALGERNON CHARLES SWINBURNE
(1837-1909),
FROM "AN INTERLUDE"

I enjoy nothing without you.
You are the prism through
which the sunshine, the green landscape,
and life itself, appear to me....
I need your kisses upon my lips,
your love in my soul.

JULIETTE DROUET (1806-1883),
FRENCH ACTRESS, TO VICTOR HUGO

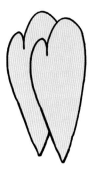

Sweet one I love you
for your lovely shape,
for the art you make
in paint and bed and rhyme,
but most because we see
into each other's hearts,
there to read secrets
and to trust,
and cancel time.

TOM MCGRATH, B.1940, FROM "REASONS"

Numberless insects there are
   that call from dawn to evening,
Crying "I love! I love!"
   But the firefly's silent passion,
   Making its body burn,
      is deeper than all their longing.
         Even such is my love....

JAPANESE TRADITIONAL SONG

He poured so gently
and naturally into my life
like batter into a bowl of batter.
Honey into a jar of honey.
The clearest water
sinking into sand.

JUSTINE SYDNEY

I need your love as
a touchstone of my existence.
It is the sun
which breathes life into me.

JULIETTE DROUET (1806-1883),
FRENCH ACTRESS, TO VICTOR HUGO

"My well-beloved is mine and I am his."

Love was their banqueting-house,
love was their wine,
love was their ensign;
love was his invitings,
love was her faintings;
love was his apples, love was
her comforts; love was his embracings,
love was her refreshing;
love made him see her,
love made her seek him.

JOHN WINTHROP (1588-1649)

I love you, not because of your noble mind and your greatness, nor in spite of your selfishness, but just because I do, and you are you, for me the sun, moon and stars to the end of time.

ELINOR GLYN (1864-1942)

You are everything I need.
You are the sun, the air I breathe.
Without you,
life wouldn't be the same.
Please never go away.
And if you go,
then don't forget
to take me with you.

BASIA

Our love is no ordinary love.
It has a history
that spans a million years.
It has a future that has no end.
It has strength and wisdom.
It is supporting and understanding.
It is growing and learning.
Our love is not bound by time,
Or space or mortal failings.

LINDA MACFARLANE, B.1953

I will love you dancing, singing, reading, making, planning, arguing. I will love you cantankerous and tired, courageous and in terror, joyful, fearful and triumphant. I will love you through all weathers and all change.

PAM BROWN, B.1928

The story of a love
is not important.
What is important
is that one is capable of love.
It is perhaps
the only glimpse we are permitted
of eternity.

HELEN HAYES (1900-1993)

I'll love you till the ocean
Is folded and hung up to dry
And the seven stars go squawking
Like geese about the sky.

W.H. AUDEN (1907-1973),
FROM "AS I WALKED OUT ONE EVENING"

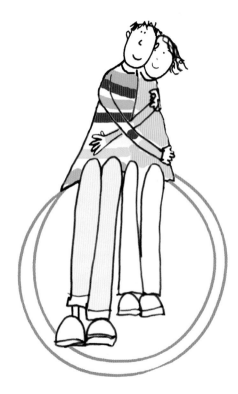

All I have is your love.
I have everything.

STUART AND LINDA MACFARLANE

Helen Exley runs her own publishing company which sells giftbooks in more than seventy countries. Helen's books cover the many events and emotions in life, and she was eager to produce a book to say a simple 'sorry'. Caroline Gardner's delightfully quirky 'elfin' cards provided the inspiration Helen needed to go ahead with this idea, and from there this series of stylish and witty books quickly grew: *Sorry*, *Go Girl!*, *I love you madly*, and *Little things mean a lot*.

Caroline Gardner Publishing has been producing beautifully designed stationery from offices overlooking the River Thames in England since 1993 and has been developing the destinctive 'elfin' stationery range over the last five years. There are also several new illustrations created especially for these books by freelance artist and designer Liz Smith.

Helen Exley Giftbooks
16 Chalk Hill, Watford, WD19 4BG, UK

www.helenexleygiftbooks.com